The Top 10 Crazy Places in our Galaxy— For Kids

Book 1 of the Top Ten Crazy Series for Kids

By James Sterling

Text & Illustrations Copyright © 2021 James Sterling

All Rights Reserved

Other images and cover used are cited at the end of this book.

Before we get to the main event, here are some fun facts about our galaxy!

- It is called the Milky Way galaxy.
- Our galaxy has a sister named Andromeda.
- The Milky Way is made up of 100 to 400 billion stars!
- The shape is a spiral with a bar for a center – like a bar of gold!
- Earth is in one of the spiral's arms in an area we call the Local Cluster.

Prepare for Launch!
10, 9, 8, 7, 6, 5, 4, 3, 2, 1...

Blast Off!

#1 Enceladus

Sixth Largest Moon of Saturn

Icy Surface of Enceladus

ENCELADUS FACTS

- Enceladus is a large ice-covered moon of Saturn.

- Enceladus was observed spewing freezing fountains of water into space!

- Enceladus has a possible capability to support life in its deep oceans.

- The surface temperature is about -330 degrees Fahrenheit. That's cold!

Enceladus ejecting fountains of icy water and gas

Surface close-up

TITAN FACTS

- Titan has oceans and lakes – but of liquid methane, not water like our oceans back home.

- Titan is an orange-colored moon of Saturn.

- Titan has the highest chance at supporting future human colonies, alongside Mars. Unlike Mars, Titan has a functional atmosphere of nitrogen and methane!

Titan's lakes of methane

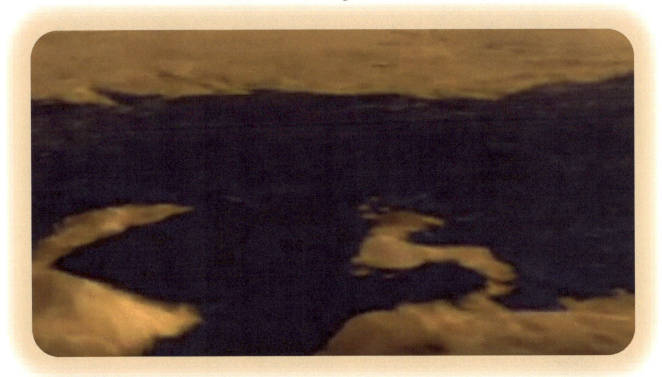

Spider Webbed Surface

Icy surface of Europa close-up

EUROPA FACTS

- Europa is an icy moon orbiting the planet Jupiter.

- Europa is covered with a spider web – but it is actually deep valleys and crevasses in the icy surface.

- Beneath the frozen surface of Europa lay deep, freezing cold oceans.

- Europa is a contender for the location with the greatest chance for life to exist on another world in our solar system.

#4 Alpha Centauri

ALPHA CENTAURI FACTS

- Alpha Centauri is the closest group of stars to our solar system.

- It is roughly four light years away which means messages from Alpha Centauri would take four years to reach us!

- Since it is the closest neighbor to us, it is the location we have the best chance of reaching with a spaceship one day!

#5 Vega
Star

VEGA FACTS

- Vega is traveling so fast through space that it is continuously tearing itself apart at the seams.

- Vega has a very high-speed planetary rotation.

- Vega was once our navigational northern pole star, around 12,000 BC, but it was later replaced. It will reclaim its status in about 11,000 years!

#6 Jupiter

Fifth Planet from the Sun

The Great Eye of Jupiter

JUPITER FACTS

- Jupiter is a massive planet – in fact, it could hold over 1,300 of our Earths inside!

- It is the fifth planet from the Sun.

- As seen in the pic above us, great storms rage on Jupiter's surface and appear as eyes since they are so enormous. It is also classified as a gas giant.

- Jupiter has 79 moons, some of them might even support life!

#7 Galactic Center

GALACTIC CENTER FACTS

- This is the heart of our galaxy.

- The center of our galaxy is a super-massive black hole.

- The material found here is many times denser than what is found in our solar system.

- Swirling around it are a cluster of some 10 million stars, mainly red dwarf stars.

#8 Venus

Second planet from the Sun

VENUS FACTS

- Venus is a planet on fire, with its toxic burning-hot atmosphere running an average of 847 degrees Fahrenheit!

- The sun rises in the west and sets in the east here.

- Venus has a poisonous atmosphere.

- Scientists would like to one day have floating labs in the skies of Venus since it is hostile to humans.

#9 Ceres

Dwarf Planet

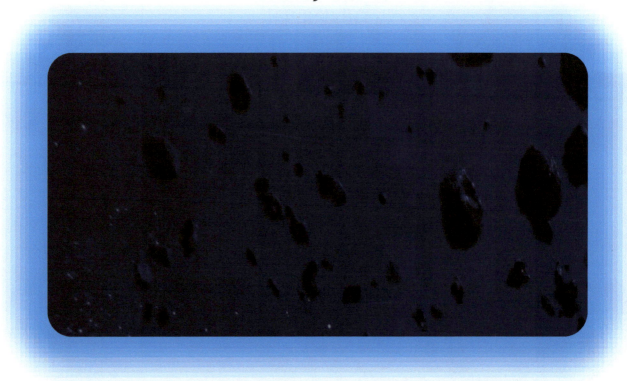

CERES FACTS

- Ceres is considered a dwarf planet and is the largest asteroid mass in our solar system!

- It is located inside our inner asteroid belt between Jupiter and Mars.

- Ceres is so massive that it has its own gravitational field

#10 Oumuamua

Interstellar Object

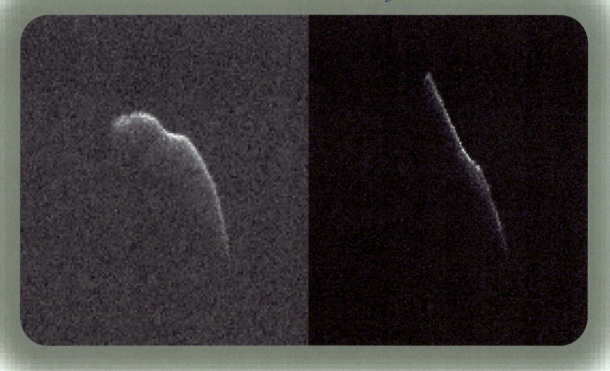

OUMUAMUA FACTS

- Oumuamua is a cylindrical comet with a 10:1 ratio of length to width, the first such elongated object in our solar system! The shape is similar to a loaf of bread.

- Oumuamua entered our solar system at 59,000 mph; increased to 189,000 mph using the gravity well of our sun; and is currently exiting our area of space at 89,000 mph!

- It is the first observed interstellar traveler that entered our solar system from the outside.

■ But where did it come from? Scientists believe such interstellar objects, such as chunks of rock, occasionally get shot out from large planetoids and other celestial bodies exploding!

■At first, this cosmic voyager set off warning bells when astronomers first spotted Oumuamua since it vaguely resembles a cylindrical spacecraft and was moving very fast. Unfortunately, it turned out to be just a large mass of rock.

There we go! Now you know the top ten craziest places in our galaxy! What a weird place we live in...

James Sterling is a long-time fiction and nonfiction writer that only recently has moved some of his work to the Amazon platform. James is originally from Illinois and then the Seattle, WA area and his nonfiction experiences cover both regions. His fiction book series are generally science fiction and/or fantasy based. To find out more about this author, visit the author page noted below. If you liked this author's work, please leave a review!

https://www.amazon.com/~/e/B08YNN1N9T

Images used on the pages listed below are courtesy of NASA and JPL pursuant to

the public domain free usage licenses and NASA/JPL commercial image licenses.

No promotion or endorsement from NASA or JPL is intended.

Link to NASA policy:

https://www.nasa.gov/multimedia/guidelines/index.html

Link to JPL policy:

https://www.jpl.nasa.gov/jpl-image-use-policy

Image pages: Cover, 1, 6, 8-9, 11-13, 15, 17, 19-20, 22, 24, 28